Has this Ever Happened to you?

Eric Moog

Dedication

I will be dedicating this book to my son Steven and my four grandchildren Madison 3 years old Kallie 7 years old Eli 8 years old and Malachi 6 months old.

Acknowledgment

This is my truth

About the Author

Have you ever felt like something extraordinary was just beyond your reach, waiting to reveal itself? Eric Moog's life has been anything but ordinary. From creepy dreams that feel too real to unexplained encounters that defy logic, Eric shares his experiences that blur the lines between reality and the unknown.

It all started when he was just a child—visions of headless figures and mysterious UFOs that seemed to follow him from his dreams into real life. As he grew older, these moments only became more intense. From strange lights in the sky over Lake Elsinore to unexplained buzzing signals from his father's homemade UFO detector, Eric's life has been filled with questions no one could answer. But every unexplained encounter left him wondering: *Why me? What does it all mean?*

For years, his past remained a mystery, especially when it came to his dreams and sightings. But now, Eric believes it's time to finally share his story.

In this memoir, he invites you into his world of wonder and curiosity, challenging you to see the unexplainable with fresh eyes. Is there something greater connecting these events? Or are they just the ramblings of an overactive imagination?

Explore the unknown with *Has This Ever Happened to You?* and decide for yourself. But beware—once you start reading, you may never see the world the same way again.

Contents

Chapter 1:
Beginnings of the Extraordinary

The most extraordinary journeys and unbelievable events often begin during the ordinary moments of our lives. Myself Eric, and it all started when I was just five years old, growing up in the peaceful streets of the lower desert of Southern California. My early years were filled with the simple joys of childhood – playing in the yard, climbing trees, riding a bicycle, finding mud puddles, and dreaming of adventures. Little did I know one particular dream would change everything. It was more than just a dream; it opened the door to something far beyond my imagination.

It was a night like any other, but as I slept, I found myself in a dark, creepy forest of oak trees standing tall and bare. The chill of winter was in the air, and an unsettling silence surrounded me. That night, I dreamt of something extremely unusual yet realistic—I was transported into a world that seemed as real as the world I was in a few seconds before. That dream forever altered the way I see the world and everything around me.

As I moved deeper into the forest, I saw something in the distance that made my heart skip a beat. About 150 or 200 feet away, there it was—a flying saucer, hovering silently above the ground with a ramp extended from its side. The sight was both mesmerizing and terrifying. Among the oak trees, the metallic craft looked completely out of place, shining in the dim light. At the bottom of the ramp stood three figures dressed in silver or perhaps white suits, but their heads were missing. This sight was quite alarming to me as a child.

Imagine yourself in this situation—alone in the woods, with darkness everywhere and a cold breeze, facing something that looks totally unacceptable but feels real. Your feelings will be exactly the same as mine. I stood still, my eyes wide with a mix of fear and excitement. I decided to run to my parents to seek comfort, desperate for reassurance. There they were—my family, all of them. But seeing them didn't give me comfort at all; it gave shivers down my spine as some of them were headless, whereas others seemed perfectly normal.

The silent, eerie presence filled me with awe, and I was unable to believe what I was watching. My heart pounded in my chest as I stared at it, unable to look away - it was completely strange and overwhelming. As my senses came back to life, I felt goosebumps all over my body.

As I looked up, the forest felt like it would crush me - trees casting long and dark shadows, making the atmosphere more tense. The flying saucer, with its ramp lowered, called out to me, inviting me to step into the unknown. I wanted to get closer, to see more, but my feet felt stuck. I was paralyzed with fear, but there was a part of me that was incredibly curious. I couldn't help myself, but this was the significant moment - the beginning of something much larger than I could ever imagine. The sight was so terrifying that I completely lost my senses. I clearly remember my grandmother holding me tightly until I caught my breath, reassuring me that it was just a dream and not a night terror, as I didn't have those as a child. However, little did I know this strange encounter in the forest would stay with me for the rest of my life as a trauma or marking the start of my journey into the extraordinary.

The next day, my mother took me downtown for a shopping trip in old Indio. As we were walking down the streets, I tried to erase the memories of yesterday's dream, licking my ice cream while holding my mother's hand, but there was something that didn't want me to forget my dream; exactly then, I saw something bizarre.

Out of nowhere, a man appeared, not a usual human being, to be very specific. A fair-height man dressed in a black suit complete with a black tie, very much like something from the 1960s. But what shocked me was that he had no head. Yes! You heard me right; he had no head. He seemed like a regular person otherwise—he had hands, and he walked with purpose, but his head was missing. There were no blood stains on his entire body, nothing suggesting he had been hurt or involved in any fight.

I looked up at my mother for some kind of reassurance with eyes full of hope. I was expecting that mom might offer some explanation to me for that strange figure that I had just seen. It could be part of a parade or a performance, something that would make sense in the daylight. But as we made eye contact, I was shocked by how calm she looked, as she didn't notice anything unusual on the street. Her face was a blank canvas, with no expressions at all. I was expecting some acknowledgment, even just a glance, but she didn't notice anything unusual on the street. Her poker face made the situation even more alarming for me, and I felt more alone than ever at that moment.

The man walked past us at a brisk pace, so close that I could feel the fibers of his coat brushing against the fibers of my shirt. It was an unexpected and uncomfortably close encounter, and I could almost sense a strange energy of electricity in the air as he walked away. I remember being so close that if he had bumped into me, I might have fallen to the ground. This encounter left me shocked and disturbed, and as the man disappeared into the crowd, I looked up at my mother again for reassurance. Weird, she was completely normal and unaware of that strange man who gave me goosebumps. It was as if he was invisible to her but not to me.

That day, my entire world changed - I realized only I was experiencing something abnormal and shady that my mother or anyone else around me couldn't feel, see, or understand.

Now, as an adult, I still question why my dreams featured a headless man and why, out of all possible things in the world, I encountered a completely unusual thing - a headless man in front of my eyes the very next day of my dream.

As a child, I had seen many unsettling things, but this was completely different and bizarre. It wasn't just any of my imagination or nightmare but a live real encounter. Even now, after so many years, I can clearly recall and think about the figure I saw in my dream and the way it resembles the man I saw live in Indio. These disturbing and unsettling experiences stayed with me forever, leaving me with a sense of wonder and confusion. Why did I dream of something so strange only to face it in reality shortly after?

This incident remains one of the most puzzling moments of my life, marking my lifelong curiosity about the extraordinary. It made me think about how children can see the world differently from adults. There may be things children pick up on, either feelings or presences, that adults can't see or feel. In my innocence, I felt like I was sensing something unusual beyond the ordinary. I felt like I had glimpsed a deeper mystery.

That day in Indio was the start of my lifelong fascination with the strange and completely unexplained world. That dream and encounter were somehow interlinked, indicating that I had finally stepped into the unknown, and this was the beginning of the extraordinary.

Chapter 2:
A Horrible Dream Comes True

For me, the 70s were a time of exploring and changing, a time that seemed to stretch out endlessly with its promising adventuring along with self-discovery. It was a period of the simplicity of youth; we didn't celebrate our memories, anniversaries, and birthdays through reminders from Facebook. We knew well who was a friend, and we kept in touch without reminders. Artificial intelligence was a myth and the internet a hoax. The warmth of friendship seemed eternal. Now, looking back and reminiscing, it all seems like a dream too good to be true. Still, my dreams weren't those that had me jolt awake with a racing heart and a soon-to-be-followed relief at the realization the nightmare was over, for I knew the dreams I had were to stay, and so they stayed. For the years to come, I was haunted as that time was full of unexpected revelations and unsettling experiences.

I was sixteen years old back in 1975. It was a time and age when I sprouted innocence, which was slowly awakening his perception. My friends, John and Mike, were my closest companions. We spent our days exploring our small Southern California town, our nights dreaming of adventures yet to come. One summer evening, a safe plan to visit the beach turned into a nightmare I had only glimpsed in my sleep. That night, I was restless. The dream came in a rush; it was alarming and unsettling.

It was not the kind of dream that left you with a sense of adventure or wonder. Instead, it was a vision of an upcoming disaster - a car crash, traumatizing and sudden, on a busy four-lane highway. The scene was filled with flashing red and blue lights and the chaotic siren noises of police and ambulance. However, the most haunting part of this dream was the woman. I saw this woman lying on her side, this blonde woman, and her eyes were cloudy blue. She was staring straight into my eyes.

I woke up with sweats all over my face, and my heart was pounding faster than ever. Dreams like these always left me unsettled, but this one was quite different yet alarming; it felt so real.

The following day, John showed up at my driveway in his old pickup truck. He casually asked me, "Eric, do you want to go to the beach?" I was reconsidering his invitation as it was a welcoming distraction from the lingering dread of the previous night's dream. He was enthusiastic and eager for a simple day of walking. John added, "I'm just going down there to just walk along the beach. That's it". I said, "Sure. Let me get dressed."

As we drove to the beach, the morning sun bathed the landscape in golden hues. This scene was a stark contrast to the darkness of my unsettling dream. As we were casually talking about random things, I thought about telling him about the nightmare that I encountered last night. I told him about the accident, the woman with the cloudy blue eyes, and how it felt so real. John listened with a casual interest; his attention was more on the drive than the details of my dream.

The beach was a familiar place - golden sand and rolling waves, where we often spent our afternoons. The parking lot was close to the beach, and John found a spot with ease, and we just parked right along the highway. We decided to park the truck and take a break before heading down to the water. The wind was brisk, so John suggested we use the truck's shell as a shelter from the gusts while we relaxed and enjoyed a joint.

Well, all of a sudden, at that moment, the truck shook violently. At first, we were confused, thinking something had hit us. But when we got out to investigate, we were met with a scene of utter chaos. The accident had occurred just a short distance away from where we parked. The scene was exactly as I had dreamt it—the familiar sight of wreckage.

The realization hit me like a cold wave. The accident was similar to my dream. The same four-lane highway, the emergency vehicles, and most scary yet alarming, the woman with the cloudy blue eyes. As we approached the wreckage, my heart sank. There, lying on the side, was the blonde woman from my dream, her eyes still open, her gaze fixed in a haunting stare. Beside her was an infant, barely clinging to life, and a young man who seemed confused but alive. The atmosphere quickly changed from peaceful to horrifying within minutes. We were one of the first to arrive at the scene, and as the chaos unfolded, it became evident that we were on our own. Most people quickly left the area as they were overwhelmed by the sight and the gravity of the situation.

Without wasting a single moment, we grabbed the sleeping bags from John's truck and used them to cover the injured. The woman was dead. The baby was also fighting for his life, but we tried to make the baby more comfortable by moving him from the harsh track to a much softer surface. John and I were left in a state of shock. The surreal connection between my dream and this tragic reality was overwhelming. The reality of what we had witnessed was far more terrifying than any dream could ever be.

So, as we were walking back to his truck, I said, "John, that dream." John, usually so composed, was visibly shaken, unable to process the coincidence. He said, "Eric, I don't want to talk about it. That screwed up our whole day." We both silently returned to the truck in silence. As we drove back home, the weight of the experience settled heavily between us. The similarity between the dream and the accident was impossible to ignore. John remained silent the entire way. John and I were closest friends through many years and we have been through many life adventures, but we never encountered anything similar to this one.

When we finally reached home, the day felt unreal and unsettling. How can my dream and this accident connect and match perfectly well? This thought was making me feel weird, yet it left me with a profound sense of unease. I couldn't shake the feeling that there was a deeper meaning to this connection, something beyond mere coincidence. The boundary between dreams and reality had blurred, revealing a troubling possibility that I might have some unusual ability to foresee events. The thought was both exciting and terrifying.

John's reaction was one of profound discomfort, and our friendship, while strong, was now strained by the weight of this shared experience. He seemed unwilling to discuss it further, retreating into a silence that spoke volumes. Whereas I was reconsidering everything and trying to understand the significance of what had just happened. It was as if I had been given a glimpse into a future that I was powerless to change. The experience was both a revelation and a curse, a burden that I would carry with me as I continued to navigate the complexities of life.

Unsettling questions swirled in my mind: Was this a mere coincidence, or was there something more sinister at play? And if my dreams could indeed foresee events, what other revelations are waiting for me? As I tried to make sense of it all, I realized that this was just the beginning. The world was filled with mysteries and unanswered questions, and my encounter with this experience was merely a glimpse into a larger, more complex reality.

One evening, as the weight of the experience became too much to bear, I decided to talk to my father about it. Our relationship had always been complicated. Growing up, my father was a strict disciplinarian, insisting that my brother and I keep busy with activities like Boy Scouts, baseball, and boxing to stay out of trouble. Despite the structured life he provided, we had our share of disagreements. But in this moment of confusion and fear, I felt the need to talk to him.

I approached him, unsure of how he would react. "Dad," I began, my voice hesitant, "I need to talk to you about something... something strange that's been happening to me." He looked up from the newspaper he was reading, his expression softening as he sensed my unease. "What is it, Eric?" he asked, his tone more gentle than usual.

I took a deep breath and began to recount the events of the past few days—the dream, the accident, and the disturbing realization that followed. As I spoke, my father's face remained calm, but there was a flicker of something in his eyes—concern, perhaps, or understanding. When I finished, there was a long silence. Finally, he put down the newspaper and turned to face me fully. "Eric," he began, his voice measured, "I want you to listen to me carefully. These dreams of yours... they may be more than just dreams. Your subconscious mind might be trying to show you something important." "But Dad," I said, my voice trembling, "why is this happening to me? I wasn't taught anything like this. Why now?" He sighed, a deep, heavy sound that seemed to carry the weight of years. "I don't know, son," he admitted, his voice soft. "Sometimes, things happen that we can't explain."

I nodded, trying to absorb his words. It was a lot to take in, and the fear and confusion still scared me. But there was also a strange sense of relief in knowing that I wasn't alone, that someone else acknowledged the reality of what I was experiencing. But for the first time since the accident, I experience a glimmer of hope. Perhaps, with the guidance of those who can understand me, I could learn to navigate this strange new world of dreams and visions.

Chapter 3:
The Unseen Presence at Huntington Beach

It was the 1970s, a time when life felt both simple and adventurous to me. People were more carefree, and everything seemed possible. The world was changing, but there was still a sense of freedom and excitement. It was a perfect time to live, explore, and be adventurous. I was young and relaxed, with a sparking excitement. The world felt like an endless adventure that I always wanted to explore. It was a bright summer day, and I was still in school, enjoying my vacation. My friend John, who was about four years older than me and already had his driver's license, decided to make the most out of this beautiful weather. He asked me, if I wanted to join him for a drive to Huntington Beach. I didn't have any plans, so I quickly grabbed my bathing suit and jumped into his truck with the camper shell.

As we made our way through the busy streets and towards the beach, I could feel the excitement building and the butterflies in my stomach. The closer we got to Huntington Beach, the more relaxed the atmosphere became. The drive to Huntington Beach felt peaceful. It was a sunny, bright day, with hardly a cloud in the sky. We weren't in any rush, so we took our time chatting about life and all the little things. It was just a day like any other. But sometimes, life has some other plans when you least expect them.

Once we reached the beach, we found a spot to park our truck. It had a camper shell, which made it a cozy place to hang out while watching the waves roll in. The beach wasn't too crowded that day, so we had our little spot. After a while, we decided to enjoy in a way that was common at the time—we lit up some marijuana and settled into the back of the truck. I remember the smell of the ocean mixing with the mild scent of marijuana smoke. It was calming, and we both were completely relaxed.

We weren't doing anything special, just enjoying the moment. The waves gently lapped against the shore, and a soft breeze blew. Everything together made a peaceful, relaxing atmosphere. But who knows, this calm was just for a short time being. Suddenly, without any warning, the truck shook violently. At first, it felt as though we had been hit, but it was more than that. We heard a terrible voice of metal crashing and screeching. Without wasting a single moment, we jumped out of the truck to see what was happening.

The scene that was waiting for us was completely chaotic and unsettling - a serious car accident had just occurred. A van was overturned on the highway, and a few other vehicles were scattered around, too. The accident had occurred just one lane away from where we were parked, and it was so close to us. In fact, a small car had stopped just inches from where we were sitting.

John and I run over to the van, not quite sure what to do. As we got closer, the scene became clear, and the horror sank in. As we reached, we saw the horrifying sight of a young couple and their baby lying on the ground. They had been thrown through the van's windshield and were lying on the road. Their bodies were injured, and it was a sight that shocked us.

The scene was a chaotic mess of broken glass and crumpled metal. It was heartbreaking and felt like everything was happening in slow motion. With no medical experience, we did what we could. We ran back to the truck and grabbed some blankets, hoping to offer some comfort. The woman, with her blue bikini top, was lying on her side with her legs twisted unnaturally. Her blue eyes were open, staring straight into mine. Her husband was lying nearby, moaning on his stomach. The baby, barely recognizable, was next to the father with a leg nearly severed. Blood was oozing out baby's mouth whenever she yelled or cried; the entire scene shattered me into pieces. It was a horrible experience.

As we stood there, still trying to make sense of it all, a strange feeling came over me. I started thinking about the night before. I had a dream. It was one of those dreams that sticks with you even after you wake up. I didn't think much of it. But now, standing here, looking at the aftermath of the accident, I couldn't forget that the dream was somehow connected to what had just happened.

In my dream, it was a warm summer night, and we were walking down a small, four-lane highway. The road was lined with familiar landmarks—a courthouse on the corner, a gas station, and even a bowling alley further down. The area was busy with traffic, cars constantly moving. I remember the street names - Sixth Street and Mountain Avenue - and the way we casually walked toward my house, which was hidden on a small side street nearby. It was the kind of night where we weren't doing much of anything, just roaming around here and there, probably after getting high, like we often did back then.

As we kept walking, the scene shifted. The usual traffic was suddenly interrupted by flashing lights and the loud sound of sirens. We came across a car accident with ambulances and police cars surrounding the area. But what stood out the most was the woman lying in the middle of the road, unnoticed by everyone around her. She was lying perfectly still, staring straight ahead as if she was looking right at us. Even though she was three lanes away, it felt like her eyes were staring right at us. It gave me an uneasy feeling like the dream was trying to warn me about something terrible that was about to happen.

Was this a warning? Had the dream trying to tell me something about what was going to happen? I replayed the details of it over and over in my mind, searching for clues, but nothing stood out. It was just a dream - at least, that's what I had told myself at the time. But now, I wasn't so sure. The similarities between the dream and the accident were too notable to ignore. I started to feel unsettled. The dream didn't give me any real warning—there was no sign that something like this was about to happen. It was as if the dream had shown me a glimpse of the future but without giving me the chance to do anything about it.

I was not able to change what was coming, and now, here I was, standing in the middle of a real-life version of what I had seen the night before in my dream.

My mind raced with questions. What did this mean? Was it just a coincidence, or was there something more going on? Could dreams really show us glimpses of the future? And if they could, what did that say about the reality itself? I didn't have any answers, I felt weird and unsure about anything around me.

I shook my head to get rid of all these thoughts and tried to offer what help I could, comforting them with the little we had. We stayed there until we could get in touch with emergency services. Fortunately, we found a doctor who had an old communication device—before cell phones were commonplace. I'm sure he got the help we needed.

Once we'd done everything we could, John and I went back to the truck, both of us in shock. The day we had looked forward to was ruined. We didn't even think about smoking marijuana anymore. Instead, we decided to take a different route back home, trying to process what we had just witnessed. The accident blew our minds completely. It was a reminder of how fragile our lives could be and how quickly things could change.

Over time, I began to accept that this was just one of those mysteries of life. Maybe the dream had been a warning, or it was just a coincidence. Either way, it left me with a feeling that there was more to the world than what we could see and touch. The accident at Huntington Beach had shaken me in more ways than one, and it had opened my mind to the possibility that we are connected to forces beyond our understanding.

After the accident, I couldn't forget the heavy feeling of guilt. It weighed on me, and I kept asking myself if there was anything more I could have done. I wanted to help, but my hands were tied. I had no real medical experience, and all I could do was offer some comfort. The worst part was seeing that helpless baby lying on its back, crying in pain. Every time the baby cried, blood oozed out from its mouth like a small fountain. The baby's foot was barely attached, hanging by just a thread of skin. It was a horrible accident. I couldn't get it out of my mind. The whole day, I felt empty and helpless, like I had failed - failed as a human being. There was nothing we could do to save them, and that sense of helplessness stayed with me for a long time. I know anyone else in my shoes would feel the same, but it didn't make the guilt any easier to bear. I was haunted by it.

Later that night, after the chaos of the day had settled, I finally had some quiet time to think. I started going over everything in my head—what had happened, the dream I had the night before, and the strange way it seemed to predict the accident. My dad and I had talked about dreams before, and he believed that dreams could be a way to guide us through life. He always told me I was sensitive and that I had a gift for having a sneak peek into something beyond the everyday world. He said dreams were a defence mechanism, a way for the mind to help us through difficult situations.

That night marked a turning point for me. I decided to take my father's advice more seriously. The dream felt like more than a coincidence - it was as if I had seen the future, but I have no power to change it. I couldn't shake the feeling in my head that maybe I could've done something helpful if I had considered the dream differently. I wondered if there had been a clue I missed, something that could have warned me about what was going to happen.

I spent hours going over the details of the dream in my mind, searching for any sign or hint that helped me to prevent the accident from happening. But no matter how hard I tried, I couldn't find anything. The dream had been so clear, but it offered no warnings or instructions. It was like watching a movie with hands tied so you couldn't stop it, knowing the outcome but unable to do anything to change it. This realization was frustrating and unsettling. It made me question the purpose of the dream. Why show me something so horrible if I wasn't meant to do anything about it? Was it just a cruel coincidence, or was there something deeper for me to consider? Even though I couldn't change what had happened, I knew this experience was opening my mind to something bigger, something I didn't fully understand yet.

I started thinking about the nature of dreams, especially ones like this that felt so real and scary. Some people call it *astral projection*, where your soul leaves your body and roams around while you sleep. Maybe that's what had happened to me. Maybe, in my dream, I had seen a glimpse of the future, something I wasn't prepared for. At the time, it was terrifying, but now I wonder if it was actually a gift. A strange and unsettling gift, but still a gift. It was like I had been shown something beyond my control, something bigger than myself. Even though it was hard to understand, it made me see things differently, and maybe that was the purpose all along. A purpose to open my eyes to the possibility that there's more to life than we realize.

I was so focused and was searching for answers constantly, replaying the dream over and over in my mind, looking for any missed sign or hidden warning. But there was nothing more to find. It was as if I had seen the whole thing twice - once in my dream and then again in real life - but I was so helpless to stop it either time. This experience really shook me and made me start questioning what's real. It felt like my life had taken a weird turn - a turn that I'm unsure about. Dreams, reality, fate - everything was starting to blur together, and I began to wonder if we're all connected to forces we can't see, or if it's just me alone in this nirvana. These forces might be guiding me or warning me, I'm not sure. But one thing that I'm sure about is they left me with more questions than answers

Chapter 4:
The Light in Lake Elsinore

Imagine this: A simple, sudden weekend getaway suddenly turns into a life-changing adventure. It sounds like something out of a movie, right? It might or might not happen to you, but for Me, it was more than just a coincidence.

It was during the summer of 1977; I was feeling bored and depressed, so I decided to drop by Mike's house to see what was going on. I knew visiting Mike would lift my spirits. I didn't think twice, put on my shoes, tied the laces, and went over. As I reached, John was already there. I felt happy to see both of them together as they were good friends of mine and were full of good vibes. After reaching, I hugged them, and to my surprise, they were planning a trip. The plan was straightforward: a weekend getaway to Lake Elsinore, where Mike's family had a beautiful vacation spot complete with a trailer, a spacious yard, a picnic table, a ski boat, a clubhouse, and much more. This gateway was a simple tradition for Mike's family, but for me, it held the promise of something extraordinary, something unusual. What began as a routine trip to the lake would soon change into an unforgettable journey, reshaping their lives in ways they could never have imagined, bringing curiosity, adventure, and lasting memories to life.

So, the journey to another extraordinary experience of my life is about to begin. We arrived at Lake Elsinore late in the evening, sometime around 9 or 10 p.m. It was dark, and the sky was heavily filled with thick clouds looming over the mountains. The night was quiet, giving our arrival a peaceful, almost calm feeling.

It was just the three of us ready for a weekend gateway followed by bottles of beer, relaxation, and maybe a few laughs.

We were completely unaware of the secrets and possibilities that the night held, but it had the potential to change everything for us. Ignoring everything, we decided to enjoy ourselves to the fullest. After unloading our beer bottles and storing them in the refrigerator, we decided to head down toward the clubhouse by the lake. The walk was short, taking us past the boat launch into a peaceful, seemingly dull night. Then, without warning, the sky above us changed. A bright light appeared, cutting through the thick cloud cover. At first, we could only see the light, not what was creating it. The clouds began to move in strange, tumbling patterns as though waves were crashing in the sky. There was a distinct line between light and dark, between white and black. Through the sky, this line between white and black was growing.

My friends and I watched in awe; we were amazed as the light moved in ways we had never seen before. It wasn't the typical glow of a streetlight or a blinking light of an airplane. This light was different - brighter and more intense, yet it didn't hurt their eyes. It bathed everything in its glow, transforming the dark night into something similar to midday. The brightness was utterly unreal, and its unusual movement captured our attention, leaving us mesmerized and curious about this mysterious phenomenon that had just happened in front of our eyes.

As we stared at the sky with complete amusement, trying to make sense of what we were experiencing, the light started to shift. It moved erratically, zigzagging through the clouds, changing directions right over Cranes Park with a speed that was far away from any reality. Each time it changed direction, it left behind a streak of light as though it was painting the sky with its wild movement. Despite the rapid and chaotic zigzagging, the light was always perfectly clear and sharp - it never faded or dimmed. It was as though we were watching a celestial show. The scene was mesmerizing, defying any logical explanation and leaving all of us fascinated.

For a moment, we were all frozen, trying to wrap our heads around what was happening. I felt something deep within myself—a mix of fear and amazement. But I was not alone in these feelings; Mike and John were equally shaken, too, though they remained mostly silent. The light seemed to be affecting us in ways we couldn't understand. It mixed emotions that were both exciting and unsettling as if we were glimpsing something that's not meant for human eyes. The air was chilled with a feeling of fear and unease, leaving us all silently struggling with the realization that we were witnessing something mysterious and not meant for us. The intensity of the moment left us speechless, each of us lost in our own thoughts but united in the shared wonder of the extraordinary.

Then, the light went upwards at a sharp 45-degree angle, disappearing as quickly as it had arrived. The erratic movements stopped, and for a few seconds, the sky was still again. It was as though the light had never been there, yet the memory of it was already embedded into our minds. We all stood there, silent, struggling to understand what we had just witnessed. For a moment, I thought it was coming out of Christ and it was the end of the world situation.

"What was that?" Mike asked with eyes filled with curiosity. But none of them had an answer.

The experience had been so surreal that it felt like we had glimpsed something beyond our understanding, something not from this world. Despite our attempts to move on, we couldn't forget the feeling that what we had witnessed was dreamy and supernatural. The ordinary surroundings of the clubhouse felt strangely dull compared to the extraordinary event we had just experienced. Our minds were stuck in the mystery of what we had seen, leaving us all feeling unsettled and deeply interested.

As we neared the clubhouse, we noticed a laundromat across the street. A car was parked out front, its hood up, and a woman was inside it. Curious and still buzzing from the encounter with the light, we decided to check what was wrong.

"Did you see that light?" I asked as we approached her. The woman looked confused, but then she nodded slowly. "I thought I saw something... bright," she said hesitantly. She wasn't as sure as they were, but she had noticed something out of the ordinary. Her car, which had refused to start before, suddenly roared to life as we talked. The moment felt strange, like something out of a movie or a dream - like the Twilight Zone. We exchanged glances, our sense of reality shaken even more. The encounter with light changed the world around us completely.

Later that night, we sat by the water, sipping our beers in silence. The sky turned back to its usual darkness, but the image of the bright light stayed with us. As we watched the moonlight reflecting the lake, we tried to make sense of it all. Was it a trick of an eye? A natural phenomenon? Or something more? I couldn't shake the feeling that this was something beyond the reality of human understanding. I found myself questioning everything I thought I knew about the world. Mike and John were equally affected. But still, none of them said a word; they all just felt it - this was not a normal lightning experience. This was something extraordinary, something that didn't belong to our world.

The strange light wasn't just a sudden moment - it stayed in our minds. Days passed, but I couldn't let it go. The light's brightness, the way it sliced through the dark sky, was something I had never seen or imagined.

Mike and John were not quite interested in talking about the experience. They all shared the moment together, but they wanted to forget it. But for me, that night in Lake Elsinore felt like a turning point, something that would be impossible to ignore. I tried to replay the scene in my head to make sense of it. What was that light? How could it move the way it did, with such speed and clarity? It felt so close, almost as if it was watching us. And that thought, more than anything, disturbed me the most.

I wasn't the type to jump to wild conclusions, but this light refused to accept all logic. If it was man-made, how could it move like that? If it was something natural, why had it felt so intelligent? These were the questions that swirled in my mind.

One afternoon, I was feeling very disturbed, unable to hold my curiosity any longer. I decided to report the experience to professionals. My father always encouraged and taught me to trust my instincts, and to me, something about this entire experience felt worth investigating. So, without wasting any further moment, I called the local sheriff's office to report what I had seen that night. To my surprise, the woman who answered the phone didn't seem all that shocked. In fact, she sounded frustrated, as though she had been dealing with calls like his all night.

"You're not the first to report it," she said bluntly. "We've had over a thousand calls about that light."

Her statement shocked me. Over a thousand people had seen the same thing? It wasn't just me, Mike, and John—it was the whole area. Whatever that light was, it wasn't some private experience. It had lit up the night for everyone around the lake, and many had been just as amazed by it as we were. The sheriff's office said they were passing all reports to the Air Force. I wasn't sure what that meant, but it didn't sit right with me. What could the Air Force do about a light like that? And why were so many people reporting the same thing? These thoughts only increased my curiosity that this was no ordinary event.

The conversation with the sheriff's office gave me some comfort. At least I knew I wasn't alone in what I just experienced. But it also raised new questions. If so many people watched it happening, why wasn't there more talk about it? Surely, something as unusual as this should have made headlines. But still, there was silence.

As the days passed, I found myself more curious about the memories of that night. Every detail felt quite important to me - the thick cloud cover, the way light passed through the sky, the weird zigzag movement, and the bright light. The more I thought about it, the more I became sure that this was not something from Earth.

However, for Mike and John, it seemed a lot easier to brush off the experience. I brought it up with them, hoping to clarify what we all seen, but they were not interested in discussing it. John, especially, seemed disturbed by the whole event. A few times, I felt that he cut me mid-sentence, refusing to talk about it further.

I understood their hesitation. The light had shaken all of us. But for me, it wasn't something I could just forget. It had left a mark, a scene that remained with me. The world was far stranger than I ever realized. I couldn't ignore it, no matter how hard I tried. Over time, I began to wonder if this event was connected to other strange experiences in my life. I had never been one to believe the unusual, but looking back, some moments stood out—moments where the ordinary had blurred into the extraordinary. The days at Lake Elsinore became a turning point in my perception of the world. The more I thought about it, the more I realized that this wasn't just a random event. It was part of a pattern, a series of strange encounters that had been scattered throughout my life. Until now, I had let go of them as coincidences of my imagination. But after that night, it was harder to ignore the connections.

I started thinking about the other past unusual events of my life: glimpses of lights in the sky, strange dreams that turned out to be real-life happenings, a feeling of being watched when no one was around, and much more. At the time, they had all seemed harmless, easy to explain away. But now, with the memory of Lake Elsinore fresh in my mind, those moments took on new meaning.

Are they all connected? I don't have an answer to my question, but it tortured me. The more I thought about it, the more convinced I became that this wasn't just a one-time event. Something had been building, slowly, over the years, and Lake Elsinore was the clearest sign of it. My friends hadn't reacted the same way. For us, the light was terrifying, yes, but it didn't seem to affect them as deeply as it affected me. Mike, always the level-headed one, had declared it as some strange military experiment. "Probably just some test flight," he said once, trying to dismiss the whole thing. But I wasn't so sure. No military technology I knew of could move like that. The Air Force might have been interested, but there was no way they could explain what I, my friends, and others experienced.

John became quieter after the incident. I could see it in his eyes — he was scared. John was scared and disturbed even more than Mike. It was as though the light had shattered something in him, some belief that the world was predictable and understandable. From that night on, John rarely spoke about what they had witnessed. The few times I tried to bring it up, John shut me down quickly.

"I don't want to talk about it," John had said on more than one occasion.

I avoid discussing this matter as talking about it has become taboo between us, hanging over our friendship like an invisible cloud. They had every right to move on, and I couldn't blame them, but for me, it wasn't that simple. That light touched something deep inside me, something that I didn't want to let go especially when I connected this incident to my past experiences. Weeks after that incident, I found myself returning to Lake Elsinore in my mind, replaying every detail. One thing, in particular, stood out to me — the moment when the light hovered over us, almost close enough to touch. I couldn't shake the feeling that we had been chosen, in some strange way, to witness this. I was pretty sure that it wasn't just a random occurrence. The light was deliberate and purposeful; it wanted to be seen.

But why?

That was the question that haunted me the most: Why did the light appear to us at that moment, on that night? There were no answers, only more questions, curiosity, and a lack of clarity. The experience at Lake Elsinore subtly changed me. I was always watching, always waiting, as if the light might return at any moment. And though it never did, the memory of it was enough to keep me looking.

For Mike and John, life returned to normal. The light became a distant memory, something they rarely spoke of. But for me, it was different. I couldn't let go. I didn't want to let go. That night had been more than just a strange experience—it had been a moment of realization, a glimpse into the unknown.

I didn't know if I would ever be able to see the light again. But even if I didn't, the experience had left its mark. I had seen something extraordinary, something beyond the scope of ordinary life. And that, in itself, was enough to change me forever.

Chapter 5:
Life in Oregon and Old Man Eric

When I first arrived in Selma, Oregon, I didn't have any idea what to expect. My life had taken an unexpected turn, relocating from Washington to this small, almost hidden part of the world. I wasn't here because of choice but necessity. It was winter, and my construction work had slowed to a halt due to the season. With nothing tying me down, I packed up and, along with my girlfriend, moved to Oregon to be there for my family. My mother, bedridden with Progressive Multiple Sclerosis, needed help, and I didn't want to leave her alone in this condition. I didn't realize at the time how much Oregon would change me.

Selma was like something out of a dream—perfect, calming, and almost otherworldly in its beauty. The air here was different and cleaner; it felt like you were inhaling the essence of the trees and the earth. The mountains that stretched beyond the horizon seemed to whisper secrets of ancient times, and the forests were so dense that they created a sense of being watched by unseen eyes. I don't know if it was just the newness of the place or something more, but Oregon felt... magical.

My days in Selma were mostly spent helping my parents and looking for work. My mom had been a fighter her whole life, but MS was a cruel disease that was killing a little bit of her every day. My father was the primary caregiver, with all the love in his heart, he would prepare my mother's meals. I did what I could to make her comfortable, but it was hard to see someone so strong become so weak. Despite the pain, though, there were moments of calm in the midst of chaos. Whenever I go out for a walk, it feels so peaceful, like breathing in a calm, fresh air and losing myself in the beauty of this landscape.

One evening, during one of my quiet, aimless walks along the winding dirt paths that crisscrossed through Selma's woods, I unexpectedly reconnected with an old friend, Jarrett. He had been living in Selma for a while, but we never got a chance to meet. Seeing him there, leaning against the side of an old, rusted truck, felt like a sudden return to something familiar—something I hadn't even realized I'd been missing.

We quickly fell back into the rhythm of our friendship, as if no time had passed since we'd last seen each other. Jarrett had a way about him—an easygoing nature that made everything feel a little lighter. I forget my thoughts and worries by his deep, rolling laughter, which echoed off the trees. We spent hours walking together, just talking—about the old days, about how different life had become, about the strange paths that somehow brought us both to this quiet little corner of Oregon. It was during one of these casual evenings that we saw something unusual in the sky that we never expected.

We were sitting outside, watching the stars, when suddenly, a red light appeared in the distance, about a mile. At first, it was just another star, no different from the others. But then something unusual caught our attention. From the left, a small blue light moved across the sky, heading straight for that star. It was strange enough to make us stop and watch. As the blue light reached the star, something unexpected happened. A tiny red light came out of the star and began moving toward the hills in the distance. The star itself still looked ordinary—a faint, twinkling dot like all the others. But then, a piercing white beam shot out, like a powerful searchlight cutting through the darkness. The beam was too far away for us to see exactly what it was lighting up, but its brightness was clear, which made us look at it. Moments later, the red light returned to the star, and the process repeated. The blue light appeared again, moving quickly, followed by the bright white searchlight. This strange cycle kept going—lights dancing in the sky, leaving us amazed and full of questions. I couldn't shake the feeling that they were looking for something specific. Minerals, maybe? I wasn't sure. But there was something about the lights that felt... unnatural.

We stood there watching for what felt like hours, but it was probably just a few minutes before the lights disappeared as quickly as they had shown up. Jarrett and I didn't talk much afterward. We just exchanged puzzled looks, both wondering silently if we had imagined the whole thing. But I knew what I saw, and I knew Jarrett saw it, too. Something weird was happening out there in the woods, and I couldn't shake the feeling that Oregon was keeping secrets it wasn't ready to reveal.

The days following that strange encounter with the lights left me with an unsettled feeling. Jarrett and I spoke about it occasionally, but after a while, we just stopped bringing it up. It was one of those things that you tuck away in the back of your mind, hoping it'll fade into the background, but it never really does. Life in Selma is quite slow, but it was not a bad thing for me at all. I found myself becoming more adaptable to the land, the sounds of the forest, and the way the air shifted as dusk turned into night. It was peaceful in a way that I hadn't experienced before, almost meditative. But that peace was often interrupted by the reality of my mother's condition. The disease had progressed to the point where she could barely move on her own, and I spent a lot of time visiting her. It was draining, emotionally and physically, but there was nowhere else I wanted to be. She needed me.

On one of my trips to the town to get supplies, I first heard about the Hippy commune. A group of older people had been living there for years, on sixty acres of land just outside Selma. It wasn't just a Hippy commune; veterans stayed as well.

One weekend, I decided to visit the commune. The road was long and winding, making it feel like I was going back in time. When I finally got there, I was amazed at how natural the place looked. It wasn't a run-down hippie commune like you see in movies. Instead, it had a rough charm, with little cabins scattered around and gardens that grew wildly and beautifully. Everything felt timeless, as if the land had been kept safe from the pressures of the modern world.

I was welcomed by a small group of residents who lived there year-round. Most were older, in their late sixties or seventies, with wrinkled faces and eyes that told stories of a life lived close to the earth. They were kind, offering me a beer and a place to sit by the fire. It didn't take long before I was introduced to Eric.

Now, Eric was different. While the others at the commune were warm and welcoming, he was more of a mystery. He was older than most of them, probably in his late seventies, with a wiry frame and a face lined with years of hard living. His eyes were sharp, though, always observing, always thinking. The others referred to him simply as *Old Man Eric*, but it wasn't just out of respect for his age. There was something about him that commanded a quiet authority without even saying a word.

Eric didn't talk much, but when he did, people listened to him. He lived on the land longer than anyone else, arriving before it had become a commune, back when it was just a piece of forgotten property in the middle of nowhere. He told stories of the early days, how he had survived on nothing but what he could grow and build with his own two hands. There was a sense of pride in the way he talked about the land as if it had become a part of him, and he was a part of it too. And the way others spoke about him, you could tell they saw him as the heart of the place.

I didn't interact much with Old Man Eric during that first visit, but something about him stuck with me. Maybe it was the way he seemed so connected to the land, or maybe it was just the sense of peace he seemed to carry with him despite his rough personality. As the weeks passed, Jarrett and I started visiting the commune more often. The more time I spent there, the more I began to understand why Eric had stayed all these years. Life off the grid gave you a sense of freedom, free from the noise of the city. The land was sustainable, providing everything they needed. The residents worked together, not out of necessity, but because they wanted to. It was a community full of love and faith.

One day, news came that Old Man Eric had passed away. I wasn't there when it happened, but as soon as I heard, I went to console other residents. Together, we quietly kicked stones and shared stories about him, feeling the weight of his absence. Then, the landowners came over and made an offer to me, as I had known the Old Man Eric for years. They asked if I would like to move into this property, take care of it, and live there. The property owners said I wouldn't have to worry about rent; all I have to care about is utilities. It felt like a way to honor Old Man Eric, and I seemed like the perfect fit to keep his place alive. However, at first, I was hesitant, but my girlfriend saw it as a good opportunity, so we gave it a chance. We packed up our belongings, moved into the house, and began cleaning out Old Man Eric's bedroom. It was a strange experience, handling the possessions of someone who had once been so full of life. We boxed everything up and moved our things in, settling into the old house. It wasn't long before strange things started happening.

One evening, while my girlfriend was in the shower, I stepped outside for a cigarette. The bathroom was on the east side of the house, and when the light was on, it softly lit up an old, worn-down shed in the yard. As I smoked, something odd caught my attention. A bright, thick beam of light the same size as the window shot out from the window of the spare room—the room where we had stored Old Man Eric's stuff.

What was strange was how the light behaved. It wasn't like normal light that spread out in all directions. This one was different. It was sharp and focused, almost like a laser, forming a straight line that cut through the dark yard. The beam angled perfectly, around 30 degrees, and pointed straight to the ground. It didn't flicker or move—it just stayed there, still, and felt completely unnatural. For a moment, I stood frozen, staring at it, trying to make sense of what I was seeing. Something was unsettling about the precision of the beam like it wasn't something that should happen on its own. I felt goosebumps all over my body, and the night, which had been calm just moments before, suddenly seemed a lot less peaceful. I couldn't shake the feeling that I just experienced something supernatural. I wasn't one to believe in ghosts, but I couldn't ignore what I just witnessed.

As time passed, strange things started happening more often. One day, I was sitting on a hilltop with some friends, surrounded by the tall oak trees that dotted the area. We were sharing a joint and enjoying the calm, quiet atmosphere when something unexpected happened. The ground beneath us began to percolate, but it didn't feel like a regular earthquake. It was as if the earth itself was breathing, pulsing in a way that felt both unnatural and somehow connected to the land.

The strange sensation spread over an area about 50-foot diameter. I had this strong feeling that water was moving beneath the surface, like something was moving deep underground. I'd never felt anything like it before. It wasn't just a physical shake—it felt almost magical yet weird like we were somehow in tune with nature in a way that didn't make sense but also felt right.

However, life in Selma wasn't all magical moments. There were struggles, too. The biggest challenge was the lack of work. With no real industry in the area and the small population, mostly retirees, finding a job was nearly impossible. I was fortunate to meet the man who had built my parents' house; he was a general contractor who gave me occasional work. But it was hit or miss, with jobs depending on whether his boss had anything available. For most of the people I met in Selma, life was tough. In times of hardship, they relied on one another and picked up odd jobs when they could.

I faced a lot of financial hardships, but my focus was on my family. My mother's illness required constant attention, and my father took on the role of caregiver. Almost every day, I visit her and am available for calls 24/7.

I lifted her from her bed, helped her down the stairs in her wheelchair, and also assisted my father in getting her where she needed to go. It was exhausting work, both physically and emotionally, but I accepted it happily. My family needed me, and that was all that mattered.

The isolation of Oregon, combined with the responsibility of caring for my mother. There wasn't much to do in town, and finding friends was quite challenging. But every now and then, I reconnect with someone from my past—like Jarett, an old drinking buddy.

Looking back at my time in Selma, I couldn't help but feel a mix of emotions. The town had brought me closer to my family and shown me the beauty of nature in a way I never experienced before. Apart from all the goodness, Oregon was also a place of struggle for me both financially, socially, and emotionally. Life in Selma was hard, but it was real. Despite the challenges, I found peace in that reality, and I am grateful for all the magical wonders that Oregon brings me.

Chapter 6:
The Metallic UFOs of Thompson Creek

It was a warm, sunny morning, right in the middle of summer, somewhere between July and August. The sun was high and shining bright, casting its golden light across the landscape. The temperature was rising, indicating the kind of hot, sticky afternoon that only summer can bring. The sky stretched out above, completely clear, without a single cloud. It was one of those perfect days that made you want to stay outside, slow down, and simply enjoy the calmness. The peacefulness of the countryside wrapped everything around itself, offering a quietness that's so rare in everyday life. The air was filled with the quiet hum of nature, and the simplicity of the moment made it feel like time itself had paused, leaving you to just breathe in the beauty of it all.

I decided to visit my friend Jarrett, who was taking care of a large property for a local mill owner, which was hidden between towering trees, but right in front was a wide, open field that stretched all the way to the road. It was roughly a football field away from where we stood at the edge of the road. On both sides of this open area there were large trees creating a natural pathway. The original owners cleared the land a long time ago, and even though it was now covered with wild grasses and weeds, you could still see its past beauty shining through. The place was quiet, peaceful, and full of possibility. It felt like a secret waiting to be revealed, with the soft whispering of the grass in the breeze and the gentle shade of the trees offering a perfect spot to dream and explore.

Jarrett was a very creative guy and a sucker for doing something, so he had big plans in his mind for the small garden that sat in front of the house. Though he knew it was a little too late in the season to plant anything substantial. As we stood there chatting, he was already talking about next year, discussing how he would organize the beds, what kinds of vegetables he might grow, and how he could improve the soil to make it more fertile. Our conversation was easy and relaxed, the kind you have when you're with someone you're comfortable with in a setting that feels timeless.

As we were talking and enjoying the most of our time, something out of nowhere, something extraordinary just happened - something that is still hard to believe.

We were casually standing there, and suddenly, our attention focused on the garden - I noticed something moving in the distance. At first, it was just a vague shape in the sky, something that didn't quite catch my attention. But it wasn't on the ground— it was floating above us, moving slowly but intentionally. As it came out from behind the trees near the road, it became clearer. To my surprise, it wasn't just one object but two, flying side by side in perfect sync.

I couldn't take my eyes off them, unsure of what I was watching. These weren't planes or helicopters; there was no sound, no familiar outline that could link them to anything made by humans. They glided smoothly through the air, almost like they were dancing. To get Jarrett's attention, I nudged him. "Do you see that?" I asked, my voice low and shaky. He looked upward, and on his very first gaze, his expression shifted from confusion to curiosity. The objects were continuously moving with steadiness, completely unbothered by the world below. My heart was beating fast with a mix of excitement and unease. What were they? Questions swirled in my mind as I hoped for answers while the two shapes floated silently in the summer sky, leaving us both in awe of this mysterious encounter.

Jarrett turned, and before I could even say another word, he spotted them, too. We stood there, completely speechless, our eyes glued to the sky as these mysterious objects floated across the sky. They weren't very high up—maybe around 200 feet, just above the tallest treetops. It felt like they were close, almost too close for comfort, and there was something strangely attractive about them.

It felt like they wanted to be seen. Yet, despite their visibility, there was an ethereal quality to them, like they existed in a world separate from ours. I couldn't shake the feeling that they could disappear at any moment, slipping away like the smoke of cigarettes. The atmosphere around us felt weird, with a sense of wonder and mystery. My heart raced, filled with a mix of excitement and uneasiness. We looked at each other, trying to process what we were seeing. It was a moment suspended in time, and all I could think was how incredible it felt to share this extraordinary experience with Jarrett, two friends united in a moment of awe.

The objects were unlike anything I had ever seen before. They were oval, elongated, but not too much—just slightly stretched out like someone had gently pulled the ends of a perfect circle. The material they were made of was even more baffling. It shimmered in a way that was almost mesmerizing, reflecting the sky and trees like a mirror. But the reflection wasn't what made it so strange. It was the way the surface of the objects seemed to move, shifting and flowing like mercury. It reminded me of that liquid metal, constantly in motion, even though the crafts themselves were moving at an incredibly slow pace—maybe only 25 miles per hour.

The objects gliding above us and under the sky were unlike anything we had ever seen or heard about. They had an oval shape that was slightly elongated - not overly stretched, just enough to make them look unique like someone had gently tugged the ends of a perfect circle. But what truly fascinated me was the material they were made of. It shimmered in an almost hypnotic way, reflecting the colors of the sky and the surrounding trees like a mirror.

Yet, it wasn't just the reflections that made them so unique; it was how the surface seemed to ripple and shift, almost as if it was alive. The movement reminded me of liquid mercury, constantly flowing and changing. As we stood there, completely shocked, I felt a mix of excitement and confusion. How could something so beautiful and strange exist in our world that I had never seen before? I could hardly believe my eyes. Every detail, from their shape to the movement of their surfaces, made it feel like we were witnessing something exceptional. The longer I watched, the more questions bubbled up in my mind. What were they? Where did they come from? And why were they here? The mystery only deepened as we continued to look at the sky, feeling like we were part of a moment that would stick in our memories forever.

For a moment, my clicked - it might be a UFO. My heart was still racing but I was determined to focus and gather every detail I could possibly can. We all had heard about UFOs, of course; who hadn't? But I never imagined that I would be able to experience something like this, especially not in this shiny, bright sunlight and this close. I tried to memorize everything—their shape, their movement, the way they seemed almost invisible, blending in with the sky and trees so perfectly that, if you weren't paying attention, you might miss them entirely.

Just when I thought things couldn't get any stranger, a third weird-looking object, same as the first two, appeared from the same tree line, gliding into view. Now, all three were floating silently across the field, one after the other, in a perfectly straight line. My heart raced, and the hairs on the back of my neck stood up - I got goosebumps. Something about the whole scene was unsettling. The weird silence, the way they moved so smoothly, so deliberately — it was like nothing I had ever seen before. This wasn't normal, not at all.

As I focused on the third one, something strange caught my eye at its base. There was a swirling energy field unlike anything I'd ever seen. It reminded me of the way heat waves shimmer off the pavement on a hot summer day, but this was different. The shimmer wasn't light and hazy; it was darker, almost like coal smoke, twisting and churning. The swirling patterns looked a bit like satellite images of storms, with clouds spinning unpredictably.

I couldn't take my eyes off it, stunned by the movement. Though I had no idea what it was, I had a gut feeling it was connected to how these objects moved. There was something both fascinating and unsettling about it. The silence of these objects, combined with this mysterious force, left me with more questions than answers and a growing sense of unease.

It was then that I noticed something even more uncomfortable — the world around us had gone completely silent. There was no sound at all. Even the objects were not making any noise—no hum, no engine, nothing. It was as if they existed in a bubble, disconnected from the natural world. The birds had stopped chirping, the breeze seemed to pause, and even the rustle of the trees faded away. It felt like the entire world was holding its breath.

And then, just as suddenly as they appeared, they were gone. They slipped behind the trees, vanishing from our sight without even a single trace. It was as if they had never been there at all, leaving behind only the weird stillness. I turned to Jarrett, still trying to wrap my mind around what had happened. "UFOs," I muttered, more to myself than to him. He nodded silently; his eyes still fixed on the spot where they had disappeared. Neither of us could fully understand what we had just seen, but we both knew it was something beyond explanation. It wasn't like anything from a movie—no flashing lights or dramatic music. They moved slowly, almost casually, as if they didn't care whether we saw them or not. They were just... there, part of our world for a moment before disappearing as mysteriously as they came.

We looked at each other with silence, uneasiness and curiosity that was very clear on our face. The moment felt like hours, but it was probably only a few minutes. My mind raced with questions. Why were they flying so low that even the naked eye could see easily? Why were they so silent? And what was that strange energy field?

Eventually, the moment faded, and the world around us seemed to wake up again. The birds began chirping, and the familiar sounds of nature returned. The sun continued its steady climb across the sky as if nothing unusual had happened. But I knew something had happened and changed.

I felt different, like I had witnessed something I wasn't meant to see — something secret, hidden from our world. It was a strange feeling, knowing I saw something beyond the ordinary, something not meant for human eyes. And yet, there was no way to forget it.

Jarrett had seen it, too, and we both stood there, quietly absorbing the weight of what we had experienced. There was no going back now. We couldn't pretend it hadn't happened. We had shared a moment that would stay with us forever, a mystery that would stay in the back of our minds, waiting for answers that might never come.

Watching those UFOs looking objects — so silent and completely out of this world typo; had opened my eyes and mind in ways that I never ever imagined or expected. No doubt this experience was quite exciting, but it was full of curiosity with a little uncomfortability. However, I never stopped asking myself questions about that, but no matter how much I invested my mind and efforts on that, I knew I would never have answers to my questions. Even at this point of my life I feel that sense of wonder, mixed with a little unease. The world around me seemed unexpected and full of possibilities that I could never think about.

Chapter 7:
The UFO Detector

My dad was always a kid by his heart all his life. He was curious, playing with his gadgets and dreaming of new inventions. Like most of man in their 40s and 50s, he wasn't the kind of guy who'd just sit back in front of the TV; he liked being busy, using his hand, and figuring out how things worked. Not only this, but he was also into Egyptology. He had this natural curiosity about the world and was always up for a challenge. So, when he learned about the strange experiences I'd been having, it was like he'd found his next big project — he wanted to help me not like a father but like a friend.

My dad was fascinated by mysteries, especially anything out of the ordinary. Many times, I saw him reading about UFO sightings or watching a show about unexplained phenomena. He'd get this spark in his eye as if he was trying to connect the dots. Sometimes, he came to me with questions that blew my mind or mentioned something he had read about electromagnetic fields or signals from outer space. But also, there are times when he just sits quietly and listens to me, nodding in a way that makes me feel he understands, even if he doesn't have all the answers. He never brushed off my experiences or treated them as silly; instead, he was genuinely curious, like he believed there was something to it.

One day, when I was chilling with my own thoughts in my room, my dad came up to me with that twinkle in his eye that meant he was up to something. "I'm going to make you something special," he said with excitement. He didn't tell me exactly what it was; he just told me that it might help with all the strange experiences I'd been having. I was super curious to know what it was, but it seemed like he wanted to keep it a surprise, so I didn't ask too many questions. Instead, I just watched as he headed out to the garage, where he did all his tinkering and inventing.

In the garage, Dad started searching through piles of old tools, wires, and random parts he'd saved over the years. He was mumbling to himself, saying words like "electromagnetic fields" and "strange signals," words that sounded scientific and mysterious to me. I didn't quite understand what he was talking about, but I could tell he was excited. In between, he held up something, examined it carefully, and then tossed it aside or added it to a growing pile of parts he thought he could use. As I watched him work, I couldn't help but feel a mix of excitement and confusion. I'd seen Dad get absorbed in projects before, but this one felt different. He was putting so much energy into it, all because he wanted to help me. I didn't know what he was building, but his determination made me feel like it was something important, something that would make me happiest.

After a while, Dad came back into the house, carrying what looked like a strange tangle of wires and bits and pieces. His face was lit up with excitement and pride, as he'd just built the world's greatest invention. "Here it is!" he said with a big smile, holding out his creation. *"A homemade UFO detector!"*

That moment felt like a dream. I couldn't help but stare at it, trying to figure out what it even was. The thing looked like some kind of science project that had gone a little wild, with parts from the smoke detector, a coil of copper wire, and a magnet all held together in a way only Dad could have come up with. It was completely handmade, for sure, and nothing like this can be found in a store. My dad was even happier than me - he was actually proud of himself as if he'd built something revolutionary, and I couldn't help but smile back.

43

The happiness on his face made me feel like he was reliving a middle school science fair moment—one where his experiment had worked out perfectly, and he just won first prize. To Dad, this little gadget wasn't just a bundle of wires, but it was a way to help me — to show me that he believed in my experiences. I couldn't help but smile, both at this weird invention and at the way Dad was so sure it would work. To him, this UFO detector was more than a device — it was a way to show he cared and wanted to support me in the most unique way he could think of.

He put the device down on the table with a smile still on his face, like he'd just invented the lightbulb or discovered something huge. I leaned in, curious but not sure what to expect. The "UFO detector" didn't look impressive—just some bits and pieces he'd put together from things around the house. There was an old smoke detector at the base, copper wire twisted carefully around, and a small magnet stuck on the side. To be honest, it looked more like a pile of spare parts than anything that could actually detect UFOs. But my dad was so excited, so proud of his creation, that I kept my thoughts to myself. He gave me a serious look and said, "You never know—maybe this thing will actually pick up something." There was a twinkle in his eye like he was half-joking but also hopeful.

We didn't really expect anything from the UFO detector, but we set it up anyway. Days passed, and it just sat there on the table as a centerpiece, completely silent and still. Honestly, I almost forgot it was even there. Then, all of a sudden, one afternoon, while I was painting in the kitchen, I heard a strange buzzing sound. I jumped, nearly dropping my paintbrush, and quickly looked around. The buzzing was coming from the UFO detector— it was turning on and off on its own! I was shocked — I couldn't believe what my eyes were witnessing. I stared at it in disbelief. Could it actually be working? The air in the room felt different like there was a slight electric charge floating around. My mind started racing, and for a moment, I thought something out of this world was happening in front of my eyes. Was a UFO actually nearby? Was I about to witness something amazing?

When I was busy with my disbelief, I noticed my dad standing at the doorway, watching me with a slight smile on his face. He didn't say anything, just sort of shrugged and walked away. Definitely do something like that just to see my reaction. He was always playful, finding little ways to catch me off guard or make me laugh. This was probably his way of adding a bit of mystery to the day, knowing I'd be fascinated by it. The more I thought about it, the more I realized he was just having fun with me, making me wonder and laugh, which was exactly what he loved to do.

At first, I felt a little disappointed, but then I couldn't help but laugh. My dad had always been full of surprises, keeping things light-hearted and fun, even with something as odd as a "UFO detector." He knew how curious and serious I was about the strange things, but he also knew I could use a little humor now and then. It was just his way of looking out for me, reminding me that no matter how weird or mysterious life could seem, there was always room to laugh.

His playful side was something I truly appreciate to this day. By setting off the detector, he turned what could've been a spooky moment into a joke we could share. I realized that his "invention" wasn't just about helping me detect anything; it was his way of showing support, blending curiosity with a little bit of silliness to remind me that things didn't have to be taken so seriously. That afternoon left me with a smile — and a feeling that, with him around, even the strangest experiences would always have a little lightness to them.

As I look back now, I realize the detector wasn't just a random device he put together with spare parts. It was more than a mix of wires, a smoke detector, and a little magnet — it was my dad's way of showing how much he cared about me. He didn't always fully understand the strange things I was experiencing, but he didn't need to. What he did understand was how important it was to me, and he wanted me to know he was there, no matter how unusual my thoughts seemed.

My dad's curiosity was always one of the things I admired most about him. Maybe he didn't buy into everything I told him, but he always listened, asked questions, and sometimes even joined in on the adventure, such as with this UFO detector. He didn't mind that it might seem silly to others; he was ready to support me in his own way, blending his humor with just enough science to make it feel real. And that's exactly what I needed — someone who could stand beside me, even if it meant jumping into the mystery just for a laugh.

The detector eventually sat quietly in our garage, collecting dust, but it never felt like a failure or a pointless project. Instead, it became a reminder of the bond we shared, of his willingness to bring a little lightness into things and keep my curiosity alive. My dad's invention wasn't just about detecting UFOs — it was about us. And knowing he would always be there to encourage me, no matter how strange my path might be, meant more than any device or gadget ever could.

All of a sudden, during the spring of 2003, in April, my father passed away just six and a half months after my mother. It was a very tough time for me and my brother. It felt like life had some tough plans for us, and it was stripping its balance, leaving us to suffer through this grief. But between that sorrow, something unusual began to happen - something that even now feels impossible to explain.

The UFO Detector that my father built for me was the main part of all this. It was a testament to his love for me. In order to keep it safe and secure, I placed that detector in the garage on the freezer after my father's death so I could always have a look at it whenever I missed him. It was fully covered in dust; I didn't think about it for months as I got busy with multiple things until the night it decided to come to life.

It was a quiet evening. Aaron, his wife, and I were talking when, suddenly, the device went off. The sound was sharp and unexpected, cutting through the silence of the house. I was the only one who knew what it was, and without explaining, I went towards the garage with my heart beating fast. I was standing there in the dim lights, staring at the buzzing detector, I felt my pulse race. It wasn't just the noise or the device itself — it was the overwhelming sense that this was more than a random malfunction. It felt like him. My father. As if, somehow, he was reaching across the veil to communicate. I told Aaron and his wife what the device was and where it had come from. Their wide-eyed disbelief mirrored my own. We checked the garage windows, the yard, everything was quiet, no bright lights, no strange phenomena outside. Just that device, humming with an energy I couldn't explain.

That was only the beginning.

After a few days, we decided to honor my parents in a way that felt meaningful. I dug a large hole in the garden, bought a young cherry tree, and mixed my father and mother's ashes together to bury beneath it. About a dozen friends and family gathered with us, standing together under the Oregon sky in order to honor our beloved parents. As we were talking, my aunt came up with an idea. She suggested we write notes — small prayers or messages and attach them to helium balloons. It seemed like the perfect gesture, a way to let our thoughts and love float toward them. We blew up the balloons, wrote our messages on them, and let them go all at once. They floated up together, rising higher and higher until we couldn't see them anymore. There wasn't any wind to push them; they just seemed to fly on their own, as if guided by something invisible and magical. To this day, my aunt, now in her eighties, still talks about that moment. It was beautiful and strangely comforting.

These experiences — my father's UFO detector, the cherry tree, the balloons — were more than mere coincidences. They were threads in a tapestry of connection, reminders that even in loss, there are ways to feel the presence of those we've loved.

These moments — my dad's UFO detector, the cherry tree, the balloons — weren't just random coincidences. They felt like pieces of a bigger picture, reminding me that even when we lose someone, there are ways to feel the presence of those we've loved. And maybe, just maybe, it was Dad's way of reminding us he was still with us.

Chapter 8:
The Strange Odor and Bigfoot

It was mid of July, and I had a few days off work, so I thought, why not head over to my buddy Jared's place? Jared and I have been friends for as long as I can remember, and it's always a good time when we hang out.

His place was perfect for relaxing and getting away from all life problems, tucked away in the countryside where it was just the two of us, a couple of beers, and nothing but wide-open fields and forested land full of peace and weird quietness. There was no one to disturb us, and we weren't disturbing anyone either - it's what we thought; nature had different plans, and neither of us had any idea about it.

One morning, after staying up a bit late, we decided to put the day to good use and cut some firewood for Jared's house. He worked as a caretaker for a large property owned by a local mill owner, and there was some BLM (Bureau of Land Management) land nearby where we could find plenty of dead and dry wood. It was nice being out there, just us, doing something productive while enjoying the peace of the forest.

We got our gear ready, loaded up the truck, and took the narrow BLM trail that wound up into the woods. The trail was rough, thick with brush, and surrounded by tall trees on all sides. But we knew if we ventured far enough in, we'd find some good wood. Jared brought his two big country dogs along; they were loyal and strong and loved running around the area. They were practically Jared's shadow, following us everywhere.

But that day, something strange happened. As soon as we got deeper into the woods, the dogs suddenly froze, perked their ears, and sniffed the air. Then, without a sound, they turned and trotted off, heading back down the trail toward the truck. Now, this was unusual. These dogs were tough; they weren't easily scared. But the way they just took off like that — with purpose but no sign of fear — was odd. Jared and I looked at each other, both of us feeling the same strange twinge of unease.

After they took off, we continued setting up the chainsaw, though both of us were a bit distracted, wondering what had made them leave. Then, it hit me: an odor. I can't even explain it properly, but it was like a mix of wet fur and something rotting as if an animal had died nearby. The smell was overwhelming and made my stomach feel weird. It was so intense that I even felt the hair on the back of my neck stand up. I didn't like it even a little bit, and neither did Jared. I turned to him and said, "Maybe we should get out of here." And to my surprise, he didn't even try to argue or brush it off. He just nodded and agreed immediately. We tossed everything back into the truck, not wasting any time.

We got out of those woods fast, both of us feeling a heavy, weird kind of weight in the pit of our stomachs. Once we were back at Jared's place, things felt a bit more relaxed, but that odd encounter stuck in our minds as a creepy moment. We didn't know what to make of it. Jared's place was near Thompson Creek, about four miles from the well-known Organ Caves. The Organ Caves were a local landmark and tourist attraction, with visitors flocking to explore the winding trails and shadowy caverns that the mountain range hid within its folds. People had been so inspired by the caves for years, drawn by their mystery and history.

We cracked open a couple of beers, hoping to settle our minds, but that terrible smell and the dog's odd behavior stayed with us. It was so out of the ordinary. I mean, we had been out in those woods plenty of times, but never had we encountered anything like this. It was as if the forest itself had changed, willing to reveal a darker side that we had never seen before. We tried to laugh it off, sharing stories and joking, but the conversation kept coming back to that weird smell and the dogs taking off.

As we talked, a recent memory popped into my mind, changing my view of things. Just a week ago, we heard something strange on the radio. A local doctor had taken his family up to the Organ Caves. They had decided to spend a day hiking on one of the main trails, which was natural, artistic, and easy to navigate. It was a safe, family-friendly spot, and plenty of tourists went there. The doctor, being the adventurous type, decided to step off the main trail for a bit to get a closer look at the forest.

While wandering a bit off the trail, he caught a whiff of a fishy smell, something so strange and powerful it turned his stomach — just like mine. He said it smelled like nothing he'd ever experienced — a thick, musty odor that had no explanation. He looked around, trying to see if maybe there was a dead animal nearby, but what he saw next shook him to his core. Standing just a few feet away was a massive creature covered in dark hair and standing on two legs. It was looking right at him, and he could see intelligence in its eyes. It wasn't an animal like a bear or anything else he knew of. The creature was massive, much bigger than any human, and it stood completely still, observing him. At that moment, the doctor said he felt pure fear like he was staring into the face of something both wild and unknown. He later claimed it was *Bigfoot* — yes, the Bigfoot that people talked about in stories, something he never thought he'd see in real life.

Terrified, the doctor quickly backed away; his heart was pounding, and he was barely able to hold himself together. He rejoined his family without saying a word about what he had seen, wanting to make sure they were safely out of the forest first. Once they were out of that forest area, he broke down in tears and told everyone what had happened to him, what he saw. His family listened in shock as he recounted the details, and it didn't take long before word spread.

Soon, the local news picked up the story, and everyone was talking about it. Some believed him, others thought he was just imagining things, but no one could deny the chill his story brought with it. Could Bigfoot actually exist and be out there, hiding in those dense, dark woods?

The doctor's story was the talk of the town for many days. It sparked a wave of curiosity, skepticism, and excitement. Everyone had an opinion, but the one thing that was stuck in everyone's mind was the same question: *was Bigfoot real?* The mystery added a strange kind of thrill to the otherwise quiet community. But it wasn't just excitement; there was an undercurrent of fear as well. This wasn't a story about something harmless or fun — this was about a creature that was large, powerful, mysterious, and unknown.

Thinking back on it, I realized there were too many coincidences. That same horrible smell, the dog's odd behavior, and the heavy feeling of something being wrong — it all added up. I turned to Jared and said, "You know, if Bigfoot's out there, we're probably in his territory. Those Organ Caves aren't far from here." Jared didn't respond at first. He just sat there, staring out toward the forest as if he could see something moving out there in the shadows. After a moment, he nodded. "Maybe we should steer clear of that part of the woods for a while," he finally said, half-joking but with an edge of seriousness.

The more we thought about it, the more it made sense. The way the dogs had taken off without a sound, not even barking, was alarming. They were big, brave dogs, protective and loyal, and they didn't get scared easily. Whatever was out there, they sensed it and wanted no part of it, and neither did we. Sitting there, we both felt that eerie sense of being watched, even though we were safely back at Jared's place.

The next day, we stayed close to home, keeping ourselves busy with chores and projects, but the memory of the woods and that awful smell wouldn't leave us alone. We kept looking toward the tree line, half-expecting to see something move out there, even though we knew it wasn't going to happen. The woods felt different now as if they were hiding secrets that neither of us wanted to find out. As the day went on, we couldn't shake the feeling that something was hiding out there, something watching us from just beyond the trees.

It's been a while since that day, but every time I'm out in the countryside or near the woods, I can't help but feel like something is out there, watching and waiting. The story of Bigfoot might just be a legend to some, but to us, it's something real, something you don't forget once you've heard about and kind of experienced something close to that. And every time I think about that strange odor in the woods and the dogs running down the trail, I wonder — was Bigfoot really out there, watching us that day? Why didn't he come in front of us? Does he really live in that place? Did our dogs feel him? My mind was spinning with thousands of thoughts and questions, but no matter how much I thought about it, I was left with nothing but more mystery. Even now, after all this time, I have no answers, and it still gives me goosebumps.

Chapter 9:
Warnings or Guides?

Have you ever woken from a dream that felt more like a riddle than a memory? My dreams often feel like this — pieces of a puzzle scattered across time or weird little movies that played in my head while I slept, teasing me with glimpses of something that are far away from my imagination. For years, I kept these dreams to myself, protecting them like secrets. Not every dream, of course; only the ones that feel important yet confusing, the ones that roam around with me like shadows, refusing to fade. These are the dreams that seem to whisper truths I can't quite understand, leaving me both interested and curious about what they can reveal.

When I woke up from the dream at first, I was very terrified but then I didn't think much of it. Consider it as - Just a bad dream - I told myself, trying to push it aside. But a few days later, the exact same accident happened, just like I had seen in my dream. The same place, the same people, the same overwhelming emotions, and the same heartbreaking result. I was shocked - goosebumps all over my body. I didn't know what to think or how to explain it. Was it just a strange coincidence, something that happened by chance? Maybe my mind had played a trick on me, making me imagine something that felt real. But what if it wasn't just that? What if it meant something more — something I couldn't understand? The whole experience left me with so many questions and no answers.

Over the years, I've had more of these kinds of dreams, or maybe visions, as they feel like more than just dreams. They come to me unexpectedly, often on calm, peaceful nights when my mind isn't filled with worries or stress. I'm not thinking about anything unusual before bed, yet these dreams arrive clear and intense as if they were meant to show me something. However, not all of them are bad. Some are just strange or confusing, but the ones that scared me stick with me the most. They stayed in my mind like precious and mysterious thoughts that I couldn't get rid of. I think of them as rare coins in a mental collection, stored away for safekeeping.

I don't talk about these dreams with anyone even my family or friends, mostly because I don't understand them myself. I just hope that someday, I'll find the answer to what they mean or why they come to me in the first place. For now, they're part of my life, popping up when I least expect them, making me wonder if they're trying to tell me something important or if they're just the reaction of an overactive mind. Either way, I can't ignore them, no matter how much I try.

Some people might call these dreams premonitions, like glimpses of the future. For me, they feel like a kind of built-in warning system, maybe even a natural tool we all have but don't completely understand. What if these dreams exist to protect us, to give us a chance to avoid danger before it's too late? What if these dreams are meant to warn us? It's a bit like seeing a cliff ahead while you're walking. If you can recognize what you've seen in time and connect it to the real world, you might be able to change your path and avoid falling. These dreams feel like that: a nudge to pay attention, a reminder that something is coming.

I don't know if everyone has this ability or if it's just something some of us notice more than others. Maybe we're all capable of these warnings, but we ignore them, brushing them off as just dreams. It makes me wonder how much we miss because we don't take the time to listen or understand what our minds are trying to tell us. Whether these dreams are a gift, a skill, or just a coincidence, I can't help but think they're trying to help in some way.

But that's the hard part, isn't it? Recognizing the dream for what it is and figuring out how it applies to real life. I've had countless dreams where I wake up feeling an urgent need to understand their meaning, yet I often come up empty-handed. The search for answers never really ends.

One dream that has stayed with me for years I still can't forget it. In the dream, there was a figure — someone or something that had no hands. The dream felt strange, almost like it wasn't happening in this world. The place was dark and covered in thick fog, with a heavy, uneasy feeling everywhere. Even though the figure never spoke, its presence was intense, almost as if it was desperately trying to tell me something.

I didn't understand what it wanted, but it left a strong impression on me. It felt like the figure symbolized loss, helplessness, or maybe even a lack of control. It seemed to be warning me about something important, but no matter how much I tried to figure it out, the meaning stayed unclear. I couldn't forget the feeling that it was connected to something big, either in my life at that time or maybe even in the future. To this day, I still think about that dream and what it could mean. Was it tied to something I was going through then? Or was it a sign of something that hadn't happened yet? I may never know the answer, but the image of that figure and the strange emotions it brought up remain with me in my mind.

Dreams like these make me wonder how much they're tied to our lives. Are they just random, or are they connected to things we can't quite see or understand yet? Whatever the case, that dream left a deep mark on me, and I can't help but feel that it had a purpose, even if I still don't fully understand what it was trying to show me.

Dreams like these have changed how I look at life. They've made me question what's real, how our minds work, and whether our lives are guided by something bigger. I can't help but feel there's more to life than what we see when we're awake. These thoughts have led me to read books by people who explore these kinds of mysteries. His work, along with others, keeps me curious and hopeful, even when answers seem out of reach.

One thing I've come to believe is that everyone has some ability to connect with something deeper, beyond the surface of everyday life. It's not a gift for just a few; it's something all of us have. For some, it might be easier to notice or use, but it's there in all of us, like a hidden part of being human that we've forgotten. It's like a muscle we don't realize we can flex.

What if we could learn to use this part of ourselves? What could we discover about the world and our place in it? Maybe we could avoid dangers, make better choices, or even understand who we are in ways we never thought possible. These dreams make me wonder if they're a way of guiding us, like clues from somewhere deep within or beyond ourselves. Even though I don't have all the answers, I feel like these experiences mean something. They encourage me to keep exploring, to pay attention, and to believe there's more to life than meets the eye. Maybe we just need to take the time to listen, to notice the signs, and to trust that there's a greater connection waiting for us to discover. It's a journey I feel we're all meant to take in our own way.

For me, dreams are like a map or, you can say, a tool for discovering myself and navigating this magical, mysterious world. They've shaped my beliefs about life and destiny, showing me that there's more to this journey than what I actually feel. They've also taught me to stay aware of my surroundings and to appreciate the little things that keep me safe and grounded.

Even at 65, I still think about what these dreams truly mean. They've made me feel connected to something larger, like an invisible thread linking us all together. I believe there are different levels of understanding, and dreams act as a doorway to those deeper places. Sometimes, I've even been aware that I was dreaming while still in the dream. It's like standing between two worlds, fully present in both at once. That feeling is both strange and exciting as if I'm catching a glimpse of something beyond ordinary life. These moments make me wonder how much more there is to explore in the hidden layers of our minds and the world around us.

Life moves forward, as it always does. People wake up, go to work, and follow their routines without much thought about the deeper mysteries of existence. But sometimes, in quiet moments, I find myself drifting into these thoughts — about life beyond Earth, other dimensions, and what our purpose might be in this universe. Are we just small pieces of a much bigger puzzle? Our dreams offer us a peek at something greater, a plan we're barely aware of. I don't have the answers, but the questions themselves keep my mind open, always wondering.

One thing I've come to believe is that dreams are more than just random images or thoughts. Whether they predict the future or not, they give us a chance to touch the unknown, to see beyond what's right in front of us. They're like windows into a reality we don't fully understand but can feel in the depths of our being. Sometimes, they're confusing, even frightening. Other times, they leave us in awe.

What I appreciate most about dreams is how they remind me there's so much more to life than what we can see, hear, or touch in our waking hours. They show us the layers of existence we often overlook in our busy routines. To me, dreams are not just strange nighttime experiences — they're a mix of wonder, mystery, and maybe even a gift from something beyond. For that, I'm deeply thankful.

Even as I carry on with my daily life, dreams stay with me, offering little glimpses of the unknown. They remind me to stay curious and to never stop questioning what else might be out there, waiting to be understood.

As I sit here reflecting on my journey, I realize how deeply my dreams have influenced not only my perspective but also how I choose to live. They've shaped me in ways I couldn't have imagined. They've taught me to approach life with caution, to trust those gut feelings that sometimes speak louder than logic, and to welcome the unknown rather than fear it.

So, I'll keep dreaming, not just while I sleep but in the way I live my life — continuously searching, learning, and growing. Each dream feels like another piece of a puzzle I'm trying to solve, even if the full picture remains out of reach for now. Perhaps, someday, everything will click into place, and the meaning behind these dreams will become clear. Until then, I'll embrace each one as it comes, treating it as a small, mysterious gift.

Dreams have taught me to appreciate the beauty of the unknown and to never stop wondering what lies beyond. They've become a quiet guide, reminding me that life is about more than just understanding — it's also about experiencing and feeling. And as long as I keep dreaming, I'll keep moving forward, one night and one step at a time.

Chapter 10:
Beyond the Ordinary

Have you ever wondered which moments genuinely define the meaning of our life? These are the obvious milestones of our entire journey – from childhood to adulthood. These moments can either be birthdays, graduations, promotions, or it could be something deeper and hidden that we often try to forget.

Whenever I ask or think about the extraordinary events of my life, I find myself stuck, unsure of which direction to take. How can I put together a story that doesn't flow in a straight line but feels more like a collection of scattered moments, each with its own weirdness, importance, and meaning? At first, I was hesitant and unsure of where to begin, what to say, and how to explain. It always felt like a task — a task that is overwhelming or like I have to navigate a maze but without any map or clear instructions. But as I started to dive deeper into the depths of my memories or life experiences, I realized that the events I buried and decided not to think about were the ones that tinged me with pain, mystery, or regret. They left permanent marks on my understanding of the world. They weren't just normal events; they were life lessons that shaped the lens through which I view life.

However, the question stayed with me forever — How will I decide which parts to share when my life starts to feel complex? Maybe the answer is in the stories that stick with me — the stories that I can't forget and that still trigger me.

Many moments in our lives shake us so deeply they leave us questioning every little bit of reality. For me, these moments are unforgettable. Still, they are like clear pictures in my mind. They weren't just random things that happened to me —- they were life-changing experiences that forced me to think differently. Take

UFOs, for example. Yes, UFOs. Not some wild stories or made-up fantasies, but real things I've seen with my own eyes. They moved silently across the sky, slow and purposeful, like they were watching over everything. It was both amazing and unsettling. You might think it sounds crazy — I get it. But once you see something like that, it sticks with you. You can't just ignore it. It makes you wonder: What else is out there that we don't understand?

These experiences changed me. They taught me that life is far more mysterious and complicated than we usually believe. The government? Either they don't know what's really going on, or they're keeping it a secret. Whatever the case, these moments pushed me to dig deeper, to question things, and to never settle for easy answers. This awareness has changed how I see the world. It's like my senses are always on high alert, searching for hidden truths. Even in my home — a place I've only had for six years — I feel it. There's this energy, like something unseen is always nearby, waiting to reveal itself if I just look closely enough. These experiences didn't make me afraid. Instead, they've made me curious, careful, and more aware of the world around me. They remind me that the unknown isn't something to ignore — it's something to explore. For me, the journey to find out the truth just started.

My frustration with all the lies we've been told has sparked something inside me, a fire that won't go out. I've often felt like I'm alone, carrying a flag and climbing a hill with no one around. It's not a path most people would choose, but for me, it's the only way. I've never been the type just to accept things blindly or follow what others expect. And even though this journey can feel lonely, it never made me angry. Instead, it made me more determined to learn, understand, and share what I've experienced. Now, you might think this all sounds a bit intense, maybe even paranoid. But

I assure you, it's not about fear or hopelessness. It's about seeing things differently. My experiences have shown me things most people don't notice: things, places, and life forms that are just beyond what we can understand. Take ghosts, for example. Many people think of them as scary or evil, but what if they're not? What if they're just another form of life, living alongside us, like Casper the Friendly Ghost — mysterious but not harmful?

However, one memory I remember clearly is my father's advice about dreams. When I was a kid, I often told my dad about my dreams — strange and sometimes scary. My dad, who was very straightforward, always supported me; he never made me feel like I was lying or experiencing something wrong. He told me to follow them even if they scare me, as there might be some kind of lesson in them.

His words stayed with me, shaping the way I see not just dreams but life. What if the things we fear the most aren't meant to hurt us but to teach us something important? What if the unknown — whether it's in our dreams, our perceptions, or the world around us — isn't something to fear but something to explore? These are the questions that keep me going.

At the time, I didn't fully understand what my father meant. But as the years passed, it became clearer. Dreams, I realized, aren't just random flashes of images; they're a window into our subconscious, a way for our minds to process the things we can't explain. Looking back, I can still recall dreams from decades ago with such clarity it feels like they happened just last night. These dreams weren't just some sort of fantasies; they were lessons, whispers from the depths of my mind. They taught me how to face my fears and how to dig for meaning when everything around me seemed like chaos. And even though I didn't follow my dad's advice to write them down, I've carried their lessons with me like hidden treasures.

But let's be real — this journey was never been a smooth one; it was a rollercoaster ride. Both in my waking life and my dreams, I've often felt set apart, like I'm seeing things others can't. It's a strange feeling, trying to explain experiences that seem beyond the ordinary. You speak, and people look at you with raised eyebrows, like you've just stepped off a different planet. It's tough, and over time, I learned to keep most of it to myself. Yes, it's isolating, but I've come to accept my role as the lone traveler.

Yet, there are moments—rare and precious—when I cross paths with someone whose path is similar to mine. These encounters, these brief exchanges, feel like finding an oasis in the middle of a vast desert. For that short while, I'm not the only one carrying the weight of unexplained experiences. We share our stories, nodding in mutual understanding, and for a moment, we connect in a way that words can't quite explain. They remind me that even in the solitude, even in the isolation, I'm not as alone as I sometimes feel. There are others out there, quietly walking their own paths, just like me.

Think about it. We're part of this Earth. We're designed to survive and thrive here. But there's so much more life around us than we can see. I'm not just talking about bacteria or microbes; I mean entities, energies, and dimensions. They're all around us, passing by unnoticed as we go about our daily lives. And that's okay. We don't need to understand everything to live meaningful lives. What we do need is courage — the courage to face the unexplainable without fear, to question without doubting ourselves, and to seek answers even when they seem out of reach.

So here I am, telling my story, not for fame or recognition, but to leave a legacy of curiosity and courage. If my experiences can inspire just one person to look at the world differently, to question and explore, then it's all been worth it. Because, in the end, it's not about what we've seen or done. It's about what we've learned and how we've grown. And for me, that growth has been beyond the ordinary.

I continued to reflect on the moments that changed my life — not just the ones involving the unknown but also those rooted in the teachings of my father. His advice often echoed in my mind: "Dreams aren't just stories, Eric. They're the language of the soul, guiding you to truths you can't yet see." As a child, I didn't understand the depth of his words, but as the years passed, they became a mantra for navigating the extraordinary events that shaped my journey.

The lessons never stopped. Each unexplained event — from the glowing orbs in the sky to the sudden, unshakable sense of being watched taught me something new about myself and the world. I learned to trust my gut feelings, to question the conventional, and to look for answers in places others might overlook. These experiences weren't just encounters with the extraordinary; they were opportunities for growth.

As I began to piece together the lessons life had handed me, it became clear that I had something valuable to share — especially with the younger generation. There's a message I've come to live by, and it's one I pass on with every chance I get: *Stay curious.* Don't let fear hold you back. The unknown isn't something to shy away from; it's where the magic of discovery happens. We tend to think that answers are the end goal, but the real beauty lies in the questions we dare to ask and the doors we choose to open.

Looking back, it's striking to see how the remarkable moments in my life — coupled with my father's wisdom, shaped me. My dad taught me early on that — life isn't about collecting answers like trophies; it's about embracing the mysteries. It's about recognizing that the universe is filled with untold possibilities. And it's our curiosity that holds the key to unlocking them. He showed me that the journey is just as important as the destination and that the real adventure lies in the searching, not the finding.

I've come to realize that our lives are shaped by what we search for and the courage we have to step into the unknown. As we get older, it's easy to think we've figured everything out, but life isn't like that. The more I explore, the more I see that there's still so much to discover. The mysteries and uncertainties aren't obstacles; they're invitations. Invitations to think more deeply, feel more, and open ourselves to experiences that go beyond what we know.

Now, as I stand here sharing my story, I feel incredibly thankful — not just for the answers I've found, but for the questions that are still out there, for the mysteries that continue to pull me forward. It's in those mysteries that the true adventure of life starts. The answers are only the beginning, but the real excitement comes from the journey, the exploration, and the constant discovery of what's hidden beneath the surface. This is what makes life truly meaningful. So, I share this with you: Keep asking, keep searching, and never stop being curious. The world is ready to show you things you've never dreamed of.

www.ingramcontent.com/pod-product-compliance
Lightning Source LLC
Chambersburg PA
CBHW051238120626
46547CB00013B/1694